Nod

Written by Celia Warren
Illustrated by Kate Leake

Nod?
To kip on?
Nod
To Sam

To Sam
Sip, sip, sip?

Dad pats Sam.

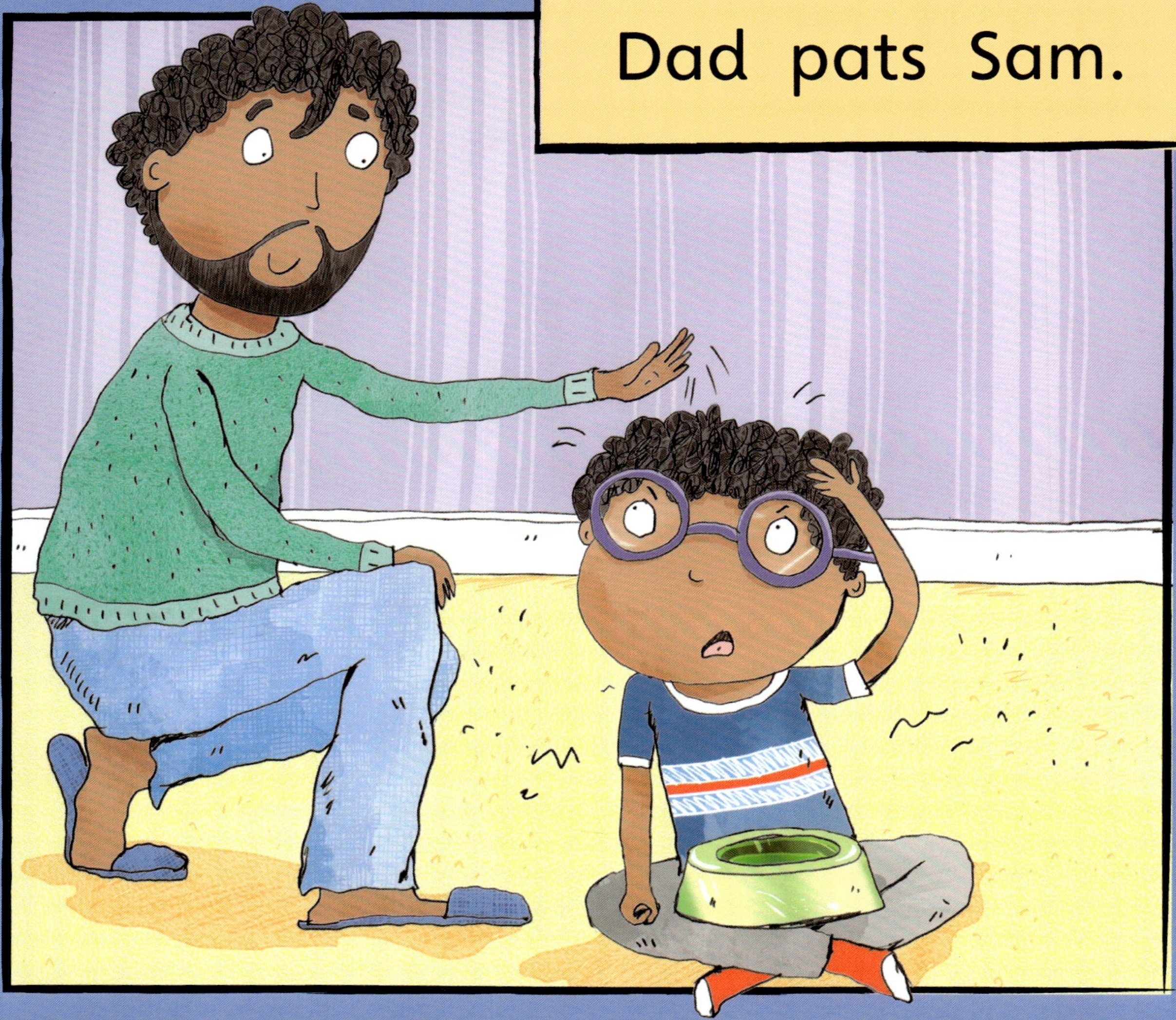

Sam is not a dog!

To Sam
Tap! Tap! Tap!
Is it a tin can?

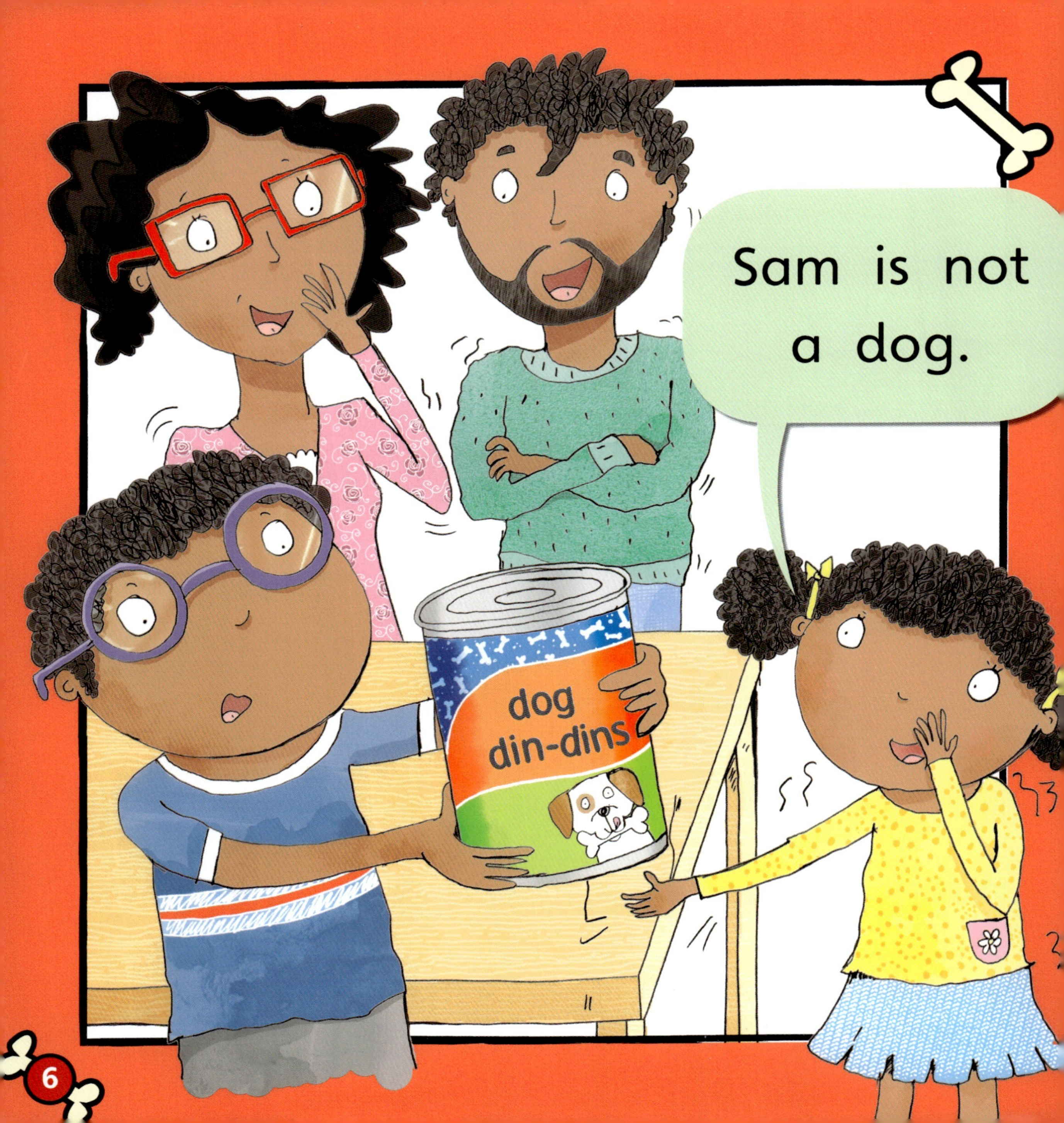
Sam is not a dog.
dog din-dins

Nod
dog
din-dins
Pit!
Pat!
Pat!
Pit!

A dog!
Nod
Sam pats and Nod naps.